Claire Macdonald's
Scottish Cookery

CONTENTS

P

CULLEN SKINK

Cullen Skink is a soup – or skink – made with Finnan haddock. It originates from the village of Cullen on the Moray Firth.

Serves 6
> 1kg/2lb Finnan haddock
> 575ml/20fl oz/2½ cups each milk and water
> 60g/2oz/¼ cup butter
> 2 onions, sliced
> about 600g/1lb 6oz potatoes, peeled and cut up
> black pepper and salt
> a good pinch of mace or nutmeg
> 30ml/2 tablespoons chopped parsley

1. Put the haddock in a saucepan with the milk and water. Bring slowly to the boil and simmer, covered, for about 4 minutes, until the fish is cooked.
2. Transfer the fish to a plate. Strain the cooking liquid into a large jug. Rinse out the pan.
3. Melt the butter in the pan, add the onion and potato and cook until the onion is soft. Add the reserved liquid, bring to the boil and simmer, covered, until the potato is cooked. Meanwhile, flake the fish, discarding the skin and bones. Keep the fish on one side.
4. Liquidise the potato mixture and return it to the rinsed-out pan. Add the fish and parsley and reheat. Season to taste with pepper, salt if necessary and mace or nutmeg. Serve very hot.

- If you cannot find Finnan haddock, use 800g/1¾lbs undyed smoked haddock.

ARBROATH SMOKIE PÂTÉ

All you need to accompany this simple, rough-textured pâté is oatcakes or plain or toasted grainy bread, and a mixed-leaf green salad if you want to serve it as a main course.

Serves 4 as a starter or 2–3 as a main course
> 1 Arbroath Smokie
> 60g/2oz/¼ cup butter, melted
> 60g/2oz/¼ cup cream cheese
> 20ml/4 teaspoons lemon juice
> plenty of black pepper
> a good pinch of cayenne pepper
> chopped parsley to garnish

1. Remove the skin and all the bones from the Smokie.
2. Break up the fish roughly with your fingers, then mix in the remaining ingredients.
3. Transfer the mixture to a serving dish or individual ramekins and chill. Garnish with chopped parsley just before serving.

- This pâté will keep well for a few days in the refrigerator. Allow it to soften before serving.

🏷 SMOKED FISH

Smoking is one of the oldest methods of fish preservation. The fish are first brined, then either hot- or cold-smoked.

Kippers are cold-smoked herrings which have usually, unnecessarily, been dyed. Look out for the paler, silvery brown, undyed kippers. The simplest way to cook a kipper is to grill it or 'jug' it – put it in a deep jug and fill with boiling water. Cover and leave for 10 minutes, then serve immediately.

Finnan haddock has its head removed, is opened out flat and cold-smoked. To cook, dot with butter, pepper well, and grill.

Arbroath Smokies are hot-smoked haddock, with bones. They require no cooking, but you can heat them through in the oven.

Traditional smoked salmon is cold-smoked, but you can now buy hot-smoked, which is served in delicious chunky pieces.

Arbroath Smokie Pâté

POACHED SALMON

When I say poached salmon, I am not referring to the salmon which arrives by stealth at the back door at midnight, but cooked salmon! Many years ago now I was taught this completely fool-proof method of poaching a whole salmon for serving cold. It doesn't matter what size the fish is, it always ends up perfectly cooked, moist and succulent. Over-cooking a salmon results in dryness which is most unpleasant, and which no amount of saucing can mask.

To cook a salmon perfectly, put the cleaned fish (with head on or off – it is up to you) in a fish kettle. Cover the fish with cold water and add some sliced onion, crushed parsley stalks, a bay leaf or two and a handful of black peppercorns. Over a moderate heat let the water reach simmering point, and then let the water simmer for exactly one minute. Then take the fish kettle off the heat and leave the fish to cool in the water. When cold, take up the fish and remove the skin. Cover the salmon with wafer-thin slices of cucumber, then brush the cucumber with sunflower oil – to prevent it from drying out – or with aspic. Serve with good home-made mayonnaise.

COD WITH MUSTARD

Cod is just one of the wide range of fish caught in the clean, cold waters that surround Scotland. The idea of combining cod with mustard originates from Orkney, and reflects the strong Norse influence on the cooking of the area. The Scottish mustard used in this recipe is made with whole mustard seeds, which gives it a light, crunchy texture. Its flavour is mild and sweet. (See page 28 for stockists.)

Serves 4

  4 thick cod fillet pieces, weighing about 900g/2lb in all
  salt and black pepper
  45g/1½oz butter
  60ml/4 tablespoons Scottish honey mustard, or
      45ml/3 tablespoons wholegrain mustard
      plus 15ml/1 tablespoon honey
  finely grated zest of 1 orange
  parsley and grated orange zest to garnish

1. Heat the oven to 180C/350F/gas 4. Arrange the cod fillets in a buttered, shallow oven-proof dish and season them with salt and pepper.
2. Mix together the remaining ingredients and spread the mixture over the cod fillets.
3. Cover with foil and bake for about 30 minutes (less if your cod fillets are smaller), until the fish is just cooked but still very moist. Serve immediately, garnished with parsley and extra grated orange zest.

 SALMON

Scottish salmon begin their life cycle in the cold freshwater streams of Scotland. It is not until their second or third year that they enter the 'smolt' stage and are ready to travel seawards to their feeding grounds. They remain at sea until they are ready to return, big and healthy, to their native rivers to spawn. It is on this journey, between February and August, that they are normally caught. Salmon which come back after just one year are known as 'grilse'. They will measure about 50cm and will weigh between 1 and 4 kilos. If they come back after two, three or four years at sea they are adult salmon, measuring 80cm to 1 metre and weighing anything from 4 to 12 kilos. Salmon that are not caught continue upstream to their spawning grounds, after which they usually perish.

Cod with Mustard

HERRINGS IN OATMEAL

One of the simplest and most traditional meals in Scotland, Herrings in Oatmeal is also one of the most nutritious. Herring is an oily fish, and used to be so cheap that it was regarded as down-market. Now, however, since over-exploitation has made it scarce, it is considered to be a great delicacy. We are told that we should include more oily fish in our diets, and what better way to do so than with this delicious recipe.

Serves 4
    4 good-sized herrings, weighing 250g/8oz each; ask the fishmonger to remove their heads and to bone them
    salt and black pepper
    60ml/4 tablespoons milk
    125–150g/4–5oz/about ¾ cup medium oatmeal
    4 rashers streaky bacon
    30g/1oz/2 tablespoons lard

1. Pour the milk onto a dinner plate and put the oatmeal on another plate beside it. Open the herrings out flat and season them well.
2. Dip each herring in milk and then in oatmeal, pressing it on as firmly as you can.
3. Using scissors, remove the rinds from the bacon and snip the bacon into narrow strips.
4. Melt the lard in a large frying pan and fry the bacon strips until crisp. Remove them from the pan with a slotted spoon and keep them warm.
5. Put the coated herrings in the hot fat (see note below) and fry them for about 2 minutes on each side. Take care that you do not overcook them.
6. Serve the herrings sprinkled with the bacon, and with boiled potatoes and a salad (see note below).

- If your pan is only big enough to cook two herrings at a time, spoon out half of the fat into a cup to use to cook the second two.
- The best salad to serve with fried herrings is one made of mixed green leaves and tomato. Use a mustardy vinaigrette dressing, which you can swirl around the pan briefly if you want to serve it warm.
- You can use mackerel, another oily fish, when herrings are not available.

COCK-A-LEEKIE

This is one of the best known of all traditional Scots recipes. It is a soup-cum-stew, consisting of chicken, leeks and prunes.

Serves 6
    1.8kg/4lb oven-ready chicken, with giblets if possible
    salt and black pepper
    1 litre/2 pints/5 cups water
    1 chicken stock cube, if needed
    1 large onion, peeled and chopped
    1 bay leaf
    a few stalks of fresh thyme, or 5ml/ 1 teaspoon dried
    500g/1lb leeks, trimmed and washed, and cut into thin diagonal slices
    18 ready-to-eat unpitted prunes
    30ml/2 tablespoons long grain rice
    30ml/2 tablespoons chopped parsley

1. Wash the chicken and season it very well inside and out. Put it, breast down, in a deep saucepan or flameproof casserole with the water. Add the giblets, if you have them, or the stock cube, crumbled. Bring slowly to the boil, skimming off any scum that rises to the surface.
2. Add the onion, bay leaf and thyme, cover tightly and simmer very gently for 1 hour, turning the chicken over halfway through.
3. Remove the giblets from the pan. Add the leeks, prunes and rice and continue to simmer gently for 15–20 minutes, or until the chicken is cooked (the juices will run clear when the chicken is pierced with a skewer).
4. Lift out the chicken onto a warmed dish. Season the broth to taste and add the parsley. Either serve the chicken and the broth separately, or cut the chicken into serving pieces or shreds and serve in the broth.

Cock-a-Leekie

ROAST GROUSE

Grouse is perhaps the best known of all game birds. It is also very good to eat, and is nicest roasted in the traditional way. Here's how to cook it:

You will need one young grouse for each person. Put an ounce of butter inside each bird and season the outside with a little salt and freshly ground black pepper. Put a rasher of bacon over each – this prevents the flesh from drying as it cooks – and roast in a hot oven for 25–30 minutes, sitting each one on a small square of freshly toasted bread for the last 10 minutes of this time.

- Serve the grouse with home-made bread sauce.
- Serve fine breadcrumbs fried in butter till golden and crisp – just a small spoonful per person.
- Game chips are a traditional and essential accompaniment – and note that bought potato crisps will not do instead! Slice potatoes transparently thinly (you can use a peeler), dry them in a teatowel then deep-fry, a few at a time, until golden.
- I like to serve a watercress salad or a cooked green vegetable, and some rowan jelly.
- Lastly, serve a thin, well-seasoned gravy.

BREAD SAUCE

Roast grouse is not complete without some good, home-made bread sauce. Use crumbs from a day-old baked white loaf, not a steamed sliced loaf.

    1 large onion, stuck with 3 cloves
    850ml/1½ pints/3¾ cups milk
    about 225g/8oz/2 cups white breadcrumbs
    60g/2oz/¼ cup butter
    salt and black pepper

1. Place the onion in a saucepan with the milk, bring slowly to the boil, then reduce the heat and simmer gently for 20 minutes. Remove from the heat, cover with a lid and leave to stand for at least an hour. Remove the onion.
2. Stir the breadcrumbs into the milk, bring to the boil and simmer for a few minutes, stirring all the time.
3. Stir in the butter, and salt and black pepper to taste.

- Bread sauce can be made ahead of time, and frozen. Do not add the butter and seasoning until you reheat the sauce. You may have to use a little extra milk to get the right consistency.

GROUSE

Above all other varieties of grouse – black grouse, wood grouse (capercaillie) and white grouse (ptarmigan) – the Scottish red grouse has the most exquisite flavour. Grouse shooting in Scotland starts on the 12th of August, known as 'The Glorious Twelfth'. Many birds shot on the 12th are whisked to London by helicopter, while still warm, to appear on the menus of London restaurants and hotels, at very high prices, that same evening. However, grouse tastes much better if it has been hung for a week, or longer if the weather is cold.

Young grouse are suitable for roasting; older birds should be casseroled or braised.

Roast Grouse

FORFAR BRIDIES

• •

The town of Forfar is known for its pasties, or bridies as they are called. The flavours and juices of the beef and onions are imparted to the pastry while cooking. Irresistibly moist and delicious, Forfar Bridies make a perfect hot or cold lunch or supper dish, to be enjoyed at any time of year.

Makes 6

500g/1lb 2oz rump steak, trimmed of fat
1 large onion, very finely chopped
85g/3oz/¾ cup shredded beef suet
30–45ml/2–3 tablespoons snipped chives
1.25ml/¼ teaspoon mustard powder
5ml/1 teaspoon salt
1.25ml/¼ teaspoon black pepper
850g/1lb 14oz made weight shortcrust pastry
   (see note below)
a little beaten egg

1. Heat the oven to 200C/400F/gas 6. Beat out the meat with a meat bat or rolling pin, then cut it up into 1cm/½ inch cubes. Put the meat in a bowl with the onion, suet, chives and seasonings.

2. Cut off a sixth of the pastry and form this piece into a ball. On a lightly floured surface, roll the ball out into a circle and cut a 20cm/8 inch circle, using a plate or cake tin as a guide. Repeat with the remaining pastry until you have six pastry circles in all.

3. Divide the meat mixture between the pastry circles, arranging it over one half of each circle and leaving a rim of 2cm/¾ inch for sealing.

4. Dampen the pastry rims with a little cold water, fold the pastry over the filling and press the edges together to seal. Crimp the edges attractively. Brush the bridies with beaten egg and make a small hole in the top of each one.

5. Place the bridies on greased baking sheets and bake them for about 45 minutes, until they are golden brown. Serve hot or cold, with vegetables or salad.

● Bought pastry is a great convenience, but it rarely tastes as good as home-made. In this recipe, for 850g/1lb 14oz shortcrust pastry use 500g/1lb 2oz/4½ cups plain white flour, 2.5ml/½ teaspoon salt, 250g/9oz/1¼ cups lard and butter mixed, and about 100ml/7 tablespoons cold water.

● Forfar bridies can also be made with lamb. Choose a good tender cut, such as leg steaks.

 HAGGIS

Haggis is the best known of all Scottish foods. It is popular with Scots, not least for the feasts of St Andrew's Day and Burns' night when it is served, traditionally, with mashed potatoes, Bashed Neeps (mashed yellow turnip or swede) and a glass of whisky. However, if you are at all squeamish you might well be put off when you read the list of its ingredients! Sheep's liver, heart and lights are minced, mixed with suet, onions, pinhead oatmeal and seasonings, then stuffed into the stomach bag of a sheep. A bought haggis will already have been cooked, and merely needs heating by immersing it in water and simmering till really hot (45–60 minutes for an average 675g/1½lb bought haggis).

Of course, if you prefer not to eat meat you can buy very good vegetarian haggis. (See page 28 for haggis stockists.)

Forfar Bridies

LAMB COLLOPS
WITH PORT AND REDCURRANT JELLY

Collops are thick slices of lean meat, in this case, lamb. Cooked here in a rich sauce, they make a fine dish for a special meal.

Serves 4

> 4 leg steaks of lamb, weighing about 500g/1lb in total
> 30ml/2 tablespoons flour
> salt and black pepper
> 85g/3oz/⅓ cup butter
> 2 onions, thinly sliced
> 225g/8oz button mushrooms, sliced
> 10ml/2 teaspoons finely chopped fresh thyme or
>   5ml/1 teaspoon dried
> 10ml/2 teaspoons cornflour
> 150ml/5fl oz/generous ½ cup beef stock
> 30ml/2 tablespoons port
> 15ml/1 tablespoon redcurrant jelly

1. Beat out the lamb steaks using a meat bat or a rolling pin. Season the flour with salt and pepper and use to coat the steaks. Melt 60g/2oz/¼ cup of the butter in a large frying pan, add the onions and fry gently until soft but not coloured. Add the mushrooms and fry for 5 minutes more, stirring from time to time. Tip the vegetables into a bowl, scooping out any liquid.

2. Melt the remaining butter in the pan, add the steaks and brown them quickly on both sides. Spread the vegetables over the steaks and sprinkle with the thyme, a little salt and plenty of black pepper. Cover the pan (you can use a tray or foil if you don't have a lid) and cook gently for 30–35 minutes, until the steaks are tender, turning them over once.

3. Blend the cornflour with a little cold water, then stir in the stock. Add this mixture to the pan and bring slowly to the boil, stirring vigorously. Add the port and redcurrant jelly and simmer for a minute or two. Serve immediately, with mashed potato and a green vegetable.

STOVIES

Stovies, a delicious, soft combination of potatoes, caramelised onions and sometimes little pieces of meat, was the meal eaten on a Monday or Tuesday, to use up the dripping and any meat left over from the weekend joint. It is a homely and comforting dish, and is guaranteed to make you come back for more.

Although this dish is often cooked on the top of the stove, here it is baked in the oven to give it a more attractive appearance.

Serves 4–6

> 1.2kg/2½ lbs old potatoes, peeled and
>   sliced 0.25cm/⅛ inch thick
> 3 onions, very thinly sliced
> 85g/3oz/6 tablespoons dripping or butter
> salt, black pepper and freshly grated
>   nutmeg
> snipped chives to garnish

1. Heat the oven to 150C/300F/gas 2. Melt 60g/2oz/4 tablespoons of the fat in a 2.3 litre/4 pint/8 cup capacity flameproof casserole, add the onion and cook gently till pale golden. Remove the casserole from the heat and transfer the onion to a plate.

2. Arrange the potato and onion in alternating layers in the casserole, seasoning each layer well with salt, pepper and nutmeg. Add 45–60ml/3–4 tablespoons water, then dot the top with the remaining fat.

3. Cover the casserole with a tightly fitting lid and cook in the oven for 2–2½ hours, removing the lid for the last hour to allow the top to brown well. Garnish with snipped chives.

● You can, if you like, add up to 225g/8oz/2 cups leftover roast meat to the casserole.

Lamb Collops
with Port and Redcurrant Jelly

CLAPSHOT

This dish, which is said to have originated in Orkney, is a delicious combination of potato and turnip (or swede, as it is called south of the border). Season your Clapshot very well with plenty of black pepper, and a good grating of nutmeg too. With plenty of cream or butter beaten in, as well as chopped chives, Clapshot makes a perfect vegetable accompaniment to any meat, game or fish.

Serves 4

- 500g/1lb floury potatoes, peeled and cut up
- 500g/1lb yellow turnip (swede), peeled and cut up
- 75ml/5 tablespoons single cream or 75g/2½oz/ 5 tablespoons butter
- 15–30ml/1–2 tablespoons snipped chives
- salt and black pepper
- freshly grated nutmeg

1. Boil the potato and turnip in separate pans, each for about 20 minutes, until tender.
2. Drain the cooked vegetables very well, put them all back in one pan and shake them over the heat to dry them off. Mash them thoroughly until they are really smooth.
3. Mix in the cream or butter and chives, and season to taste with salt, plenty of black pepper and a grating of nutmeg. Continue to mash over the heat. Turn the mixture into a warmed serving dish and serve immediately, to accompany a main dish.

- Alternatively, you can put the Clapshot in an oven-proof dish, sprinkle with grated Scottish cheddar cheese and slip under a hot grill, or in the oven, until the cheese is bubbling.

SKIRLIE

Skirlie, made with oatmeal and onions, is one of the most delicious dishes and it complements a whole variety of meats. When I make Skirlie I flavour it with lemon rind and fresh thyme. We are never stuck for thyme here on Skye because, as well as being cultivated extensively, thyme grows wild in most parts of Scotland.

Serves 4–6

- 2 onions, roughly chopped
- 85g/3oz/6 tablespoons dripping or butter
- about 150g/5oz/¾ cup medium oatmeal
- finely grated zest of 1 lemon
- 10ml/2 teaspoons chopped fresh thyme or 5ml/ 1 teaspoon dried
- salt and black pepper

1. Melt the fat in a frying pan, add the onion and cook over a medium heat until it is well browned.
2. Stir in enough oatmeal to make a fairly thick mixture, add the lemon zest, thyme and salt and pepper to taste, then continue to cook and stir for about 7 minutes, until cooked. Serve hot, to accompany a main dish.

- Skirlie can also be used as a stuffing for chicken. Cool the mixture immediately after adding the oatmeal, then use in the usual way.

OATMEAL

There are several grades of oatmeal, from pinhead, through rough and medium, to fine and even superfine. Each grade has its own particular uses. The oatmeal I use the most is pinhead, which is made by cutting the oat kernels in half and sifting away the meal. It has a nutty texture and is delicious used in many recipes. If you live out of Scotland and find it difficult to buy oatmeal, try looking in a health food shop.

Rolled oats are made by removing the husks from the grains and then steam-softening and rolling them flat. Rolled oats keep well because they have been heat-treated, but oatmeal should not be kept too long or it will go rancid.

Oatmeal is very good for you because it reduces cholesterol in the blood and so reduces the risk of heart disease.

Skirlie

CLOOTIE DUMPLING

A Clootie Dumpling is a fruity pudding steamed in a cloot – a cloth. It smells most enticing! As long as you prepare the cloth properly with a coating of flour, the pudding won't stick to it. The 'skin' of the pudding, produced by boiling it in the cloth, is considered by some to be the best part. We serve Clootie Dumpling with a creamy egg custard sauce flavoured with vanilla, but you could flavour it with ginger or orange – or both.

Serves 8

150g/5oz/1¼ cups self-raising flour
115g/4oz/2 cups fresh white breadcrumbs
170g/6oz/1½ cups shredded suet
150g/5oz/1 cup soft dark brown sugar
250g/9oz/1½ cups mixed sultanas, raisins and currants
30ml/2 tablespoons marmalade
5ml/1 teaspoon ginger
5ml/1 teaspoon cinnamon
grated zest of 1 orange and 1 lemon
15ml/1 tablespoon golden syrup or treacle
2 eggs, beaten
about 170ml/6fl oz/¾ cup milk

1. In a large bowl, mix all the ingredients together.
2. Dip a large, squarish cotton cloth (you may have a suitable tea towel) into boiling water, then spread it in a large bowl. Sift a layer of flour onto the cloth.
3. Put the dough on the prepared cloth, then draw up the corners of the cloth and tie securely with string, allowing extra space for the pudding to expand.
4. Put a trivet or an upturned flan tin in a large saucepan, put in the pudding and pour in enough boiling water to cover. Cover with a lid and boil steadily for 3 hours, topping up with more boiling water when necessary.
5. Lift the pudding out onto a plate. Untie the cloth and peel it back carefully, so as not to damage the 'skin'. Turn the pudding onto a plate and sprinkle it with a little caster sugar. Serve immediately, with custard.

● You can, if you prefer, cook the pudding in a well-greased 1.7 litre/3 pint/8 cup capacity pudding basin. Grease a square of foil and fold a pleat across the middle of it. Tie the foil to the basin with string, winding it twice around the basin, under the rim, and then looping it over the top to make a handle.

BRAMBLE AND APPLE CRUNCH

Serves 4–5

750g/1½lbs cooking apples, peeled, cored and thinly sliced
250g/8oz blackberries
30ml/2 tablespoons caster sugar
60ml/4 tablespoons orange juice
5ml/1 teaspoon cinnamon
60g/2oz/½ cup wholemeal flour
115g/4oz/1½ cups rolled oats
85g/3oz/generous ½ cup soft light brown sugar
85g/3oz/6 tablespoons butter

1. Heat the oven to 190C/375F/gas 5. Put the apple in a buttered oven-proof dish with the blackberries, sugar, orange juice and cinnamon.
2. Mix the flour, oats and brown sugar, then melt the butter and stir it in. Spoon the mixture over the fruit.
3. Bake for 50–60 minutes, until the topping is browned and the apple is cooked. Serve hot or warm, with cream or ice cream.

PORRIDGE

Porridge is essentially Scottish. It used to be made in the morning, cooled, then cut into slabs to eat throughout the day.

The best porridge is a world away from rolled oat porridge made with milk. It is made with a combination of medium and pinhead oatmeal, which is put in a saucepan with cold water and stirred over the heat until it boils. It is then removed from the heat, covered with a lid and left overnight, then salted and reheated in the morning.

To serve 3, use 115g/4oz/⅔ cup oatmeal, 550ml/1 pint/2½ cups water and 2.5ml/½ teaspoon salt.

Serve with milk, cream, buttermilk or yogurt, and honey, brown sugar or treacle.

Clootie Dumpling

QUEEN MARY'S TART

The Queen Mary referred to here is, of course, Mary Queen of Scots, and this tart, with its moist, fruity filling, is supposed to have been much enjoyed at Holyrood Palace. I can quite imagine it would have been! (See picture on page 29.) Serve it with tea or coffee, or as a dessert.

Serves 6
> 340g/12oz frozen puff pastry, defrosted
> 45ml/3 tablespoons apricot jam
> 85g/3oz/⅓ cup soft butter
> 85g/3oz/6 tablespoons caster sugar
> 3 large eggs, beaten
> 115g/4oz/1⅓ cups ground almonds
> finely grated zest of 1 orange and 1 lemon
> 30ml/2 tablespoons orange juice
> 85g/3oz/½ cup sultanas

1. Heat the oven to 200C/400F/gas 6. Roll out the pastry and use it to line a 23cm/9 inch tart tin. Prick the base lightly with a fork and spread with the jam.
2. Beat together the butter and sugar until pale and fluffy. Beat in the beaten eggs, a little at a time, adding a little of the ground almonds if the mixture begins to curdle. Stir in the almonds, orange and lemon zest, orange juice and sultanas. Spoon the mixture into the pastry case and spread it evenly.
3. Bake for 10 minutes, then reduce the oven temperature to 180C/350F/gas 4 and bake the tart for a further 25 minutes, until the filling is risen and firm.
4. Serve warm or cold, plain or with cream.

● You can vary this recipe by using marmalade in place of the apricot jam, and brandy in place of the orange juice in the filling.

BUTTERSCOTCH TART

This pudding is the first that I remember eating when I arrived in Scotland. The Scots have a very sweet tooth, and that is probably why I feel so at home in this country! This tart is scrumptious eating for those similarly inclined. The buttery vanilla flavour of the butterscotch filling is somehow enhanced by the soft meringue top. But many a butterscotch tart is spoiled by insufficient simmering of the filling, so make sure you simmer the mixture really well to cook out the raw flavour of the cornflour.

Serves 6
> 280g/10oz made weight shortcrust pastry
> 150g/5oz/1 cup soft light brown sugar
> 75ml/5 tablespoons cornflour
> 170ml/6fl oz/¾ cup milk
> 30g/1oz/2 tablespoons butter
> 1.25ml/¼ teaspoon vanilla essence
> 2 large eggs, separated
> 115g/4oz/½ cup caster sugar
> 2.5ml/½ teaspoon cream of tartar

1. Heat the oven to 200C/400F/gas 6. Roll out the pastry and use to line a 20cm/8 inch tart tin. Prick the base with a fork and bake blind (see note below). Reduce oven to 150C/300F/gas 2.
2. Mix the brown sugar and cornflour with 45ml/3 tablespoons of the milk. Bring the rest of the milk to the boil in a small pan. Pour it onto the sugar mixture, stirring, then return the mixture to the pan. Bring slowly to the boil, stirring all the time, then cook for 3 minutes, stirring vigorously.
3. Off the heat, stir in the butter, vanilla and egg yolks, then stir over a gentle heat for 2 minutes. Pour into the pastry case.
4. Whisk the egg whites until stiff but not dry. Whisk in the caster sugar, a spoonful at a time, and the cream of tartar. Pile the meringue on top of the tart and bake for about 30 minutes, until the meringue is crisp and lightly browned. Serve warm or cold, plain or with cream or ice cream.

● To bake blind, line the pastry case with grease-proof paper and fill with dry beans. Bake for 10 minutes, then remove the paper and beans and bake for a further 5 minutes.

Butterscotch Tart

CALEDONIAN CREAM

This delicious mixture of curd cheese and marmalade is quick and simple to make, and is a perfect accompaniment to orange segments or strawberries. If you prefer, you can put it in the freezer until it is lightly frozen, stirring it occasionally with a fork to keep it smooth.

Serves 4–6
    450g/1lb/2 cups curd cheese
    115g/4oz/⅓ cup fine cut marmalade
    30ml/2 tablespoons caster sugar
    30ml/2 tablespoons whisky or brandy
    15ml/1 tablespoon orange juice

Mix all the ingredients together and chill well.

EDINBURGH FOG

Serves 5
Whip 280ml/½ pint/1¼ cups whipping or double cream until it is just thick. Add 5ml/1 teaspoon vanilla essence, 50g/2oz/⅔ cup crushed ratafia or amaretti biscuits, 30ml/2 tablespoons chopped blanched almonds and 30–45ml/2–3 tablespoons icing sugar, to taste. Add 30ml/2 tablespoons brandy, if you like, then divide the mixture between 5 small glasses. Chill the dessert until you are ready to serve it.

CRANACHAN

Cranachan is one of the best sweet summer fruit recipes in the whole repertoire of traditional Scottish dishes. Whipped cream is mixed with honey, whisky and raspberries. The final ingredient is toasted oatmeal, and I use pinhead oatmeal because its texture is so very complementary to the smooth and creamy sweet. Some fold it through the cream, but this tends to turn it soft. I prefer to scatter a spoonful onto each serving of Cranachan just before it is served.

Serves 4
    60ml/4 tablespoons pinhead oatmeal
    280ml/10fl oz/1¼ cups double cream
    30ml/2 tablespoons whisky
    about 45ml/3 tablespoons liquid honey
    250g/8oz raspberries

1. Put the oatmeal in a small, dry frying pan and toast it over a gentle heat for 20–30 minutes, shaking the pan from time to time, until the oatmeal is lightly browned.
2. Meanwhile, whip the cream until it is thick but not stiff. Add the whisky, and honey to taste.
3. Reserve a few of the best raspberries for decoration and fold the rest gently into the cream.
4. Spoon the mixture into 4 glass dishes and chill until you are ready to serve.
5. Just before serving, sprinkle the toasted oatmeal on top of the cream and decorate with the reserved raspberries.

SCOTCH WHISKY

Whisky is undoubtedly Scottish, though there is one line of thought which suggests that the art of making whisky was brought to Scotland by Irish monks. Whisky used to be distilled in many a Scottish farm kitchen, and was a task well within the capability of any servant.

The taste of whisky varies distinctly depending on the area in which it is made. For example, the whiskies from Islay are more dense in flavour than those made in Speyside. To my taste, the lightest – and most delicious – is Highland Park, made in Orkney.

The art of making whisky is a delicate one, and whisky connoisseurs can even detect the subtle differences between the whiskies of one area, caused merely by the water being drawn from different rivers.

Cranachan

DUNDEE CAKE

Home to the old family firm of Keillors, who are renowned for their bitter orange marmalade, Dundee is better known for this cake. You can spot a Dundee Cake from afar, by its rings of whole almonds pressed into the top. This is one of the best examples of Scottish baking, and nobody bakes like the Scots. (See picture on page 29.)

225g/8oz/1 cup soft butter
225g/8oz/1 cup caster sugar
5 large eggs, beaten
280g/10oz/2½ cups self-raising flour
115g/4oz/⅔ cup raisins
115g/4oz/⅔ cup sultanas
115g/4oz/⅔ cup currants
60g/2oz/¼ cup mixed peel
60g/2oz/¼ cup glacé cherries, rinsed, dried and halved (optional)
finely grated zest of 1 orange and 1 lemon
15–30ml/1–2 tablespoons sherry
a good pinch of salt
85g/3oz/1 cup ground almonds
a little milk, if necessary
60g/2oz/⅓ cup whole blanched almonds

1. Heat the oven to 150C/300F/gas 2. Grease a 23cm/9 inch round cake tin, line it with greaseproof paper and grease again.
2. Using a hand-held electric whisk if you have one, beat the butter and sugar together until light and creamy. Beat in the beaten eggs, a little at a time, adding a little of the flour if the mixture begins to curdle.
3. Mix in the dried fruit, peel, cherries (if using), orange and lemon zest and sherry. Sift the flour and salt onto the mixture, add the ground almonds and fold in. Add a little milk, if necessary, to give a soft dropping consistency.
4. Turn the mixture into the tin. Level the top and arrange the whole almonds over the top. Bake for about 2 hours, until the top is lightly browned and a skewer inserted in the middle comes out clean. You may need to cover the cake with foil to prevent it from over-browning.

BROONIE

Broonie is a traditional Orkney gingerbread, and its name is derived from the Norse word 'bruni', meaning 'thick bannock'. It is one of several traditional Scottish gingerbreads. Broonie keeps well in an airtight tin. Serve it plain or buttered.

170g/6oz/1½ cups plain flour
2.5ml/½ teaspoon bicarbonate of soda
10ml/2 teaspoons ground ginger
170g/6 oz/1 cup medium oatmeal
85g/3oz/⅔ cup dark soft brown sugar
85g/3oz/⅓ cup butter
30ml/2 tablespoons black treacle
280ml/10fl oz/1¼ cups buttermilk or yogurt
1 egg, beaten
85g/3oz/½ cup raisins (optional)

1. Heat the oven to 180C/350F/gas 4. Thoroughly grease a 10x20cm/4x8 inch loaf tin and sprinkle it lightly with flour.
2. Sift the flour, bicarbonate of soda and ginger into a large bowl. Stir in the oatmeal and sugar, breaking up any lumps of sugar.
3. Melt the butter and treacle together in a pan, add the buttermilk and then the beaten egg. Pour this mixture onto the dry ingredients and stir them well together. Stir in the raisins, if using.
4. Pour the mixture into the prepared tin and bake for 50–60 minutes, until just firm in the middle.
5. Leave it to cool in the tin for 15 minutes, then turn it out onto a rack and leave to cool completely. Wrap the Broonie and store in an airtight container for 3 days, to allow the flavour and texture to develop. Serve plain or buttered.

● You can embellish the Broonie with grated orange or lemon rinds, and you can add a little cinnamon with the ginger.

Broonie

OATCAKES

Each area of Scotland has its own traditional shape and recipe for oatcakes. The recipe I like the best, which was taught to me by an Aberdonian, uses half and half oatmeal and wholewheat flour. Oatcake mixture dries out quickly and becomes difficult to handle, so if you want to make a lot it is best to repeat the recipe until you have as many as you need.

  60g/2oz/⅓ cup medium oatmeal
  60g/2oz/½ cup wholemeal flour
  a good pinch bicarbonate of soda
  4 good pinches salt
  15ml/1 tablespoon melted lard
  2–3 tablespoons boiling water

1. Mix the dry ingredients in a bowl. Using a round-bladed knife, stir in the melted lard and enough hot water to make a firm, soft dough.
2. Sprinkle your table with oatmeal and roll out the dough to a thin circle, turning it, rubbing it with oatmeal and neatening the edges frequently. Cut the circle into quarters, sixths or eighths. (These are called 'farls'.) Leave them to dry for 30 minutes. Meanwhile, either heat the oven to 180C/350F/gas 4, or heat up a griddle.
3. To oven cook, place the oatcakes on an ungreased baking sheet and bake for 15–20 minutes, turning them over halfway through the cooking time.
4. To cook on the griddle, place the oatcakes on the hot griddle and cook gently until they curl at the corners. Turn them over and cook until firm.
5. Cool the oatcakes in a toast rack, or propped up against a food can, so that they become crisp. When cold, store in an airtight container. Serve with pâté, cheese, honey, jam or just butter for breakfast, lunch, supper or a snack.

SCOTS PANCAKES

Scots Pancakes are a most comforting feature of the tea table. They can be made on a griddle, a frying pan or the hotplate of a Rayburn or Aga (if you lift the lid of the coolest hotplate half an hour before cooking). Stack them on a plate and serve them warm with butter and a good home-made jam or jelly, and they will disappear like the proverbial snow off a dyke!

Makes about 24
  150g/5oz/1¼ cups plain flour
  60g/2oz/¼ cup caster sugar
  5ml/1 teaspoon bicarbonate of soda
  7.5ml/1½ teaspoons cream of tartar
  a pinch of salt
  1 large egg, beaten
  170ml/6fl oz/¾ cup milk
  oil for greasing

1. Sift together the dry ingredients into a bowl and blend in the egg and milk. If possible, leave to stand for a few hours.
2. Oil the surface of the Aga, or the heated griddle or pan. Drop dessertspoonfuls of the mixture onto the hot surface. When bubbles appear all over the surface and the underside is browned, turn the pancakes over using a palette knife, and allow them to brown on the second side.
3. Keep the cooked pancakes warm in a cloth on a plate while you cook the remainder.

SCOTTISH CHEESE

There are cheeses being made throughout Scotland these days which rival, or in many cases surpass, those being made in mainland Europe. These cheeses are made from cows', sheep's and goats' milks, and range from hard, cheddar-type cheeses, through soft and creamy, brie-like cheeses, to the Scottish curd cheese called Crowdie, which dates back to an 11th-century recipe.

Scottish cheeses are made with a stunning range of flavourings, mustard, herbs, whisky, claret and garlic to name but a few. Many cheeses, including crowdie and goats', are smoked.

It isn't easy to find Scottish cheeses out of Scotland, although you might find a slightly better selection around Burns' night. Luckily, cheeses can be ordered and sent to you directly from Scotland. (See page 28 for stockists.)

Scots Pancakes

SHORTBREAD

This Shortbread is made in a round with a crimped or notched edging which is said to symbolise the sun's rays. You must use the best butter, and I like to put in a small amount of ground rice, which gives a pleasing, slightly granular texture. You can flavour the basic shortbread in a number of ways – with cinnamon, grated orange or lemon rinds, chopped nuts or chopped stem ginger, for example.

Shortbread is usually eaten with tea or coffee, but it is also good as an accompaniment to a light, fruity pudding, such as a mousse or fool, or with berries and cream.

> 170g/6oz/¾ cup good butter, at room temperature
> 85g/3oz/6 tablespoons caster sugar
> about 200g/7oz/1¾ cups plain flour
> 60g/2oz/⅓ cup ground rice
> extra caster sugar, for sprinkling

1. Heat the oven to 150C/300F/gas 2. Blend the butter and sugar together with the fingertips of one hand, then gradually work in the flour and ground rice until you have a soft and pliable dough. Press it gently into a ball.
2. On a lightly floured surface, roll or press the dough into a round of about 18cm/7 inches. Lift it onto a baking sheet, then crimp the edges, prick it with a fork and mark it into 8 segments.
3. Bake the shortbread for about 40 minutes, until it is light golden brown in colour. As soon as you take it from the oven, sprinkle it with caster sugar. Cool on the tray for a few minutes, then transfer it to a rack to cool completely.

● Pitcaithly Bannock is a very old traditional shortbread, made particularly for Christmas and weddings. To the basic recipe above, add 30g/1oz/¼ cup crushed flaked almonds and 2 knobs of stem ginger, finely chopped, working them in along with the flour. You can decorate the shortbread with little pieces of stem ginger before baking.

PARLIES

These simple ginger biscuits are said to have been served to the Scottish parliament, hence the name Parlies.

Makes 15
> 125g/4oz/½ cup butter
> 125g/4oz/⅓ cup black treacle
> 125g/4oz/¾ cup soft light brown sugar
> 200g/7oz/1¾ cups plain flour
> 10ml/2 teaspoons ground ginger

1. Heat the oven to 170C/325F/gas 3. Melt the butter and treacle together in a pan. Remove from the heat and stir in the remaining ingredients.
2. Press the mixture into a greased rectangular tin measuring 18x28cm/7x11 inches. Bake for about 20 minutes, until evenly browned.
3. Mark the hot biscuits into 15 squares, leave to cool in the tin until firm, then transfer to a rack to cool completely.

TABLET

This Scottish confectionery tastes similar to fudge but has a firmer texture.

Makes about 700g/1½lbs
> 500g/1lb 2oz/2¼ cups granulated sugar
> 170ml/6fl oz/¾ cup water
> 60g/2oz/¼ cup butter
> 45ml/3 tablespoons sweetened
>   condensed milk

1. Put all the ingredients in a heavy saucepan and stir over a gentle heat until the sugar has completely dissolved.
2. Bring the mixture to the boil and simmer it until it reaches the soft ball stage (see note below), or measures 116C/240F on a sugar thermometer.
3. Remove the pan from the heat and set it on a board. Allow the mixture to cool for a few minutes, then beat it with a wooden spoon for about 5 minutes, until it becomes opaque. Pour it into a buttered 18x28cm/7x11 inch tin. Mark it into squares before it sets.

● To test for soft ball, drop a little of the mixture into a cup of cold water and let it cool for a few minutes. It should roll into a soft ball between your finger and thumb.

Shortbread

ATHOLL BROSE

One of the Dukes of Atholl is said to have filled a well with this whisky liqueur in order to stupefy and capture his enemy.

Makes 70cl / 25fl oz / 3 cups
 85g/3oz/½ cup medium oatmeal
 45ml/3 tablespoons liquid heather honey
 425ml/15fl oz/2 cups whisky

1. Put the oatmeal in a bowl with 225ml/8fl oz/ 1 cup water and leave to stand for 1 hour.
2. Strain the mixture through a fine sieve into a wide jug. Press with the back of a spoon to extract all the liquid. Save the liquid and discard the oatmeal.
3. Stir in the honey, then pour through a funnel into a 70cl bottle. Add the whisky and stopper the bottle securely. Shake well before serving.

COOK'S NOTES

Metric, imperial and US cup measures are given for each recipe. Please follow just one method of measuring, not a mixture.

All spoon measures are level. We have used special measuring spoons, which are widely available.

The accuracy of the cooking times we have given in these recipes depends on the oven being preheated to the specified temperature before use.

British name	US equivalent
caster sugar	fine granulated sugar
treacle	molasses
plain flour	all-purpose or cake flour
cornflour	cornstarch
bicarbonate of soda	baking soda
sultanas	seedless white raisins
glacé cherries	candied cherries
double cream	heavy cream
curd cheese	smooth cottage cheese
stock	bouillon
yellow turnip/swede	rutabaga
grill	broil
frying pan	skillet

SCOTTISH FOOD SUPPLIERS

If you have any difficulty obtaining Scottish foods, there are several food companies in Scotland that have mail order systems, and will deliver quickly and efficiently.

The Achiltibuie Smokehouse (*tel:* 01854 622353, *fax:* 01854 622335, *e-mail:* sifsalmo@globalnet.co.uk, www.summerislesfoods.com) in Ross-shire sells smoked salmon, cured in a variety of ways to give mouth-watering flavours. Also available are organic smoked salmon, smoked fish and Highland meats, and an exceptionally tasty smoked Highland cheese.

The Gourmet's Lair (*tel:* 01463 225151, *e-mail:* sales@gourmetslair.co.uk, www.gourmetslair.co.uk) is a family-run shop in Inverness, specializing in cheeses – they offer over 150 varieties – as well as Scottish biscuits, cake, tea and coffee, sauces, mustards and chutneys, honey and preserves and a wide range of Scottish beers, wines and spirits.

Isabella's Preserves (*tel:* 01651 806257, *fax:* 01651 806232, *e-mail:* isabellaspreserves@btinternet.com, www.isabellaspreserves.co.uk) are made in Aberdeen-shire to the original recipes of Isabella Massie. Her delicious Scottish mustard relish, mild and sweet in flavour, has a marvellous crunchy texture produced by using whole mustard seeds.

Isle of Skye Seafood (*tel:* 01471 822135, *fax:* 01471 822166, *e-mail:* sales@skye-seafood.co.uk, www.skye-seafood.co.uk) sells fresh fish and shellfish caught by local fishermen. A speciality is their Scottish wild salmon: after a slow cure with rum and brown sugar, it is smoked over oak chips from whisky barrels then hand sliced.

Letterfinlay's Larder (*tel:* 01397 772957, *fax:* 01397 772181, *e-mail:* RYP15@aol.com) has an impressively wide range of Scottish cheeses, delicious smoked game, meats, salmon and fish, superb handmade chocolate truffles, cakes and oatcakes and more.

Macbeth's (*tel and fax:* 01309 672254, *e-mail:* enquiries@macbeths.com, www.macbeths.com) is a butcher and gamedealer with a high reputation. Their haggis is made to a family recipe, using a natural skin, and has an excellent, spicy flavour.

Macsween of Edinburgh (*tel:* 0131 440 2555, *fax:* 0131 440 2674, *e-mail:* haggis@macsween.co.uk, www.macsween.co.uk), well-known for his excellent haggis, also makes an extremely good vegetarian haggis using pulses, vegetables, nuts and oatmeal. You can phone Macsween and ask for your nearest supplier of Macsween haggis.